Weapons and Warriors

Frederick Wilkinson

Macdonald Educational

Contents

How to use this book

This book tells you about the fighting man and his weapons, from the flint-headed spear to the laser-sighted rifle. It does not cover sea warfare, air warfare or the history of artillery. Look first at the contents page to see if the subject you are looking for is listed. For instance if you want to find out about the Ancient Greeks, you will see that they are to be found on page 12. The index will tell you how many times a particular subject is mentioned and whether there is a picture of it. The blunderbuss, for example, you will find on page 29. The glossary explains the more difficult terms.

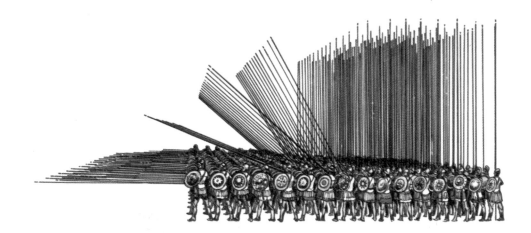

Introduction

Early man had to fight to survive. He fought wild animals which attacked him or which he had to kill for food. He also fought against other men who tried to drive him away from his hunting grounds.

The first weapons

At first he used any stick or stone to defend himself, but gradually he learned how to make better weapons. He sharpened the end of the stick to make a point so that he could stab.

He found that some kinds of stone, particularly flint, could be shaped into sharp pieces that would cut. Later still he found out how to make bows, so that he could throw his sharp pointed sticks a longer distance—as arrows.

Arms and armour

Eventually the wandering hunters settled and lived in villages. These grew into towns, until there were enough men to form an army in times of trouble.

Over the centuries the soldier's weapons improved and his equipment became more and more complicated. Some men became weapon makers and others made armour. The story of arms and armour is really about competition between these two groups of craftsmen.

Weapon makers might design a new type of sword but the armourers would then try to make armour that the sword could not pierce. The weapon makers would then design another kind of weapon to break through the new armour.

Workers in metal

The making of armour reached its peak in the fifteenth and sixteenth centuries. Swords, daggers and other edged

Early man's weapons were wooden branches or stones that he found.

Today's soldier can knock out tanks using rockets or guided missiles.

weapons were made by men called *cutlers*, whilst *armourers* and mail-makers supplied the armour. All these craftsmen were very skilled, able to work steel and iron into all shapes.

Most of this shaping was done by hand with the metal being hammered on wooden or metal blocks. Some armourers set up their workshops by the side of rivers and so were able to use the running water to turn wheels and so drive mechanical hammers.

Rich men could have their suits of armour made to measure, but ordinary armours were designed so that they could be easily adjusted to fit most men.

Gunmakers

Gunpowder, in use in China nearly a thousand years ago, reached Europe in the Middle Ages. Firearms became common from the 16th century. At first they were simple and could be made by armourers or blacksmiths themselves.

As they became more complicated they needed special skills and knowledge and some workers began to make only firearms. These men were the first gunmakers. Most guns included the work of several craftsmen who made the different parts; the barrel, the wooden stock, the firing mechanism and all the fittings. Until about 1850 almost all the gunmaker's work was done by hand but from then on more and more machines were used to produce firearms.

Modern warfare

The contest between weapons and armour is still going on today. For many years the tanks and armoured fighting vehicles seemed to rule the battlefield, but today a single infantryman can destroy a tank with a missile.

The armourer is beating out a metal plate over a wooden stake.

A 17th century Dutch gunmaker makes the wooden stock for a gun.

7

Stone and wood

Flint is a kind of stone which is common to many parts of the world. It is often found in chalk. If a block of flint is struck at certain points it will split and thin flakes will break off.

Early man gradually discovered how to split and shape these pieces of stone until he could make them into knives, spear heads and arrow heads. Large pieces were fitted on to wooden shafts and served as axes.

Improved stone weapons

Flint tools and weapons in the early Stone Age were fairly simple and rough, but gradually the workers learnt how to polish and shape the flint pieces.

Arrow heads were carefully made with a short neck which could be used to attach them to the wooden or reed shafts. The shaft was carefully split, the arrow head inserted and then bound in place.

Flint or a similar stone was used over the centuries by warriors throughout the world. The Aztecs of Central America used pieces of obsidian, a black rock which comes from volcanoes. They would fix pieces along the edge of a wooden sword to give it a vicious cutting edge. On the islands of the Pacific many of the warriors used pieces of stone to make large axes. The Maoris of New Zealand used wide, flat axes made of stone or bone.

The aborigines of Australia also fashioned weapons of stone, but they came to use new materials, such as glass, which the English settlers brought with them.

The coming of metal weapons

When smiths began to make metal weapons in about 3500 BC, it was obvious that they were much better, stronger, sharper and longer lasting than those made of flint. Fewer and fewer flint weapons were made although flint was still used for arrow heads—a flint-tipped arrow was worth much less than one of bronze and so mattered less if it was lost.

Recent tests have shown that flint arrows are almost as good as those of steel and penetrate as well. Peoples like the Indians of North America continued to make flint arrow heads right up to this century.

Primitive peoples decorated rocks and caves with pictures of hunting scenes.

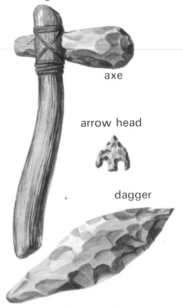

axe

arrow head

dagger

Above: flint could be shaped to make weapons and tools.

Right: some warriors in New Guinea still use weapons of stone and wood, but many now own metal weapons.

Bronze and iron

In about 3500 BC, somewhere in the Middle East, it was discovered that if one kind of rock became very hot it turned into a liquid. When this liquid cooled it set hard again. Copper was the first metal to be used but it was rather too soft to make really good weapons.

The discovery of bronze

Someone else discovered that if a little bit of tin was mixed in with the copper, the new metal, bronze, was much harder. Gradually the smiths learnt how to make furnaces, mix metals and fashion moulds of clay or stone.

The metal was melted, poured into the moulds and left to cool and set hard. The mould was then opened and the metal shape carefully turned out and polished. The smiths made all kinds of bronze weapons.

Bronze was in use in Egypt and South-West Asia by 3500 BC. It reached Britain about 1500 BC.

Although ancient flint workers were very skilled, they could not make swords. The trouble was that long, thin pieces of flint break very easily. When the smiths learnt

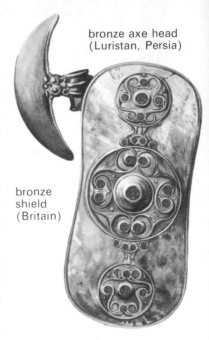

bronze axe head
(Luristan, Persia)

bronze
shield
(Britain)

Above: bronze could be easily cast or shaped.

Below: Egyptians battle with Hittites at Kadesh.

iron sword
and dagger
(Germany)

Above: iron was more difficult to work but gave swords and daggers a sharper edge.

how to make bronze they were able to cast long blades and for the first time warriors could have long swords.

Weapons made of copper or bronze were much better, and stronger than those made from flint. They were, however, both rather soft metals and if a bronze or copper blade was used very often it soon became blunt.

The use of iron

Eventually metal workers discovered the secret of working with a new metal, iron.

At first the secret of working iron seems to have been known only to the Hittites, a race of people living in what is now part of Turkey. Gradually other races learned the secret and the knowledge of iron working seems to have become widespread by about 1200 BC. The use of iron reached Britain in the fifth century BC.

Iron was a more difficult metal to work and it needed a much higher temperature to melt it, but it was much harder, tougher, and it kept sharp longer.

Often the early swords had blades of iron and hilts of bronze. Although iron was used for weapons, bronze was still used for the manufacture of arrow heads and armour, for this metal was easier to work and shape.

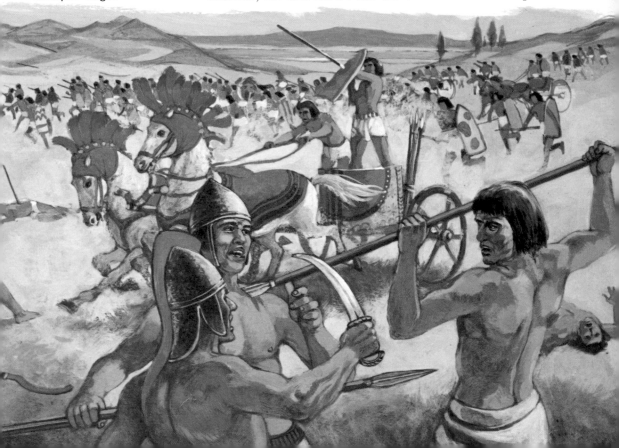

The Greeks

Ancient Greece was made up of several small states, often under very different kinds of rulers. Two of the most important states were Athens and Sparta. Often the two states were enemies, but sometimes, when they were threatened with danger, they joined forces against a common enemy, such as the mighty Persian empire.

At the Battle of Thermopylae in 480 BC the Spartans fought the Persians to the last man.

Sparta was a state which trained all its young men in the arts of war and believed that war and fighting was the most important of all occupations.

The greatness of Greece

After the Persian wars ended in 449 BC, many Greek states flourished. The thinkers, architects, soldiers and writers of Athens were the admiration of later Western civilization. The city states were conquered by Philip II of Macedon in 338 BC. Philip's son, Alexander the Great, founded an empire that stretched from Egypt to India.

The hoplite

The Greek warriors were called *hoplites*. They carried great, round shields of wood covered with bronze. They were armed with a long, bronze-pointed spear and a short, slightly curved sword called a *kopis* which was carried on the left. The hoplite usually wore bronze armour which was made up of a breast and backplate, which we call a *cuirass*. Some also had two springy metal shin guards that we call *greaves*.

Their helmets were beautifully made and were beaten out of a single piece of bronze. Some completely covered the head with only an opening for the eyes and nose. Other helmets had wide, downward sloping rims and these were popular with the cavalry.

Recognition in battle

In a battle it is obviously important to be able to recognize one's friend and for this reason the Greek warriors often fitted crests to the top of their helmets. These were made of horsehair or thin metal and were sometimes in the shape of animals. They also painted big patterns on the front of their shields.

helmet

spears

kopis

shields

Some Greek helmets covered the head and had crests so that the wearer could be recognized. The shields often had painted patterns.

THE PHALANX

Greek armies fought in a formation known as the *phalanx.* This was a solid block of hoplites all holding their long spears forward. The phalanx drove back the enemy by sheer weight and strength.

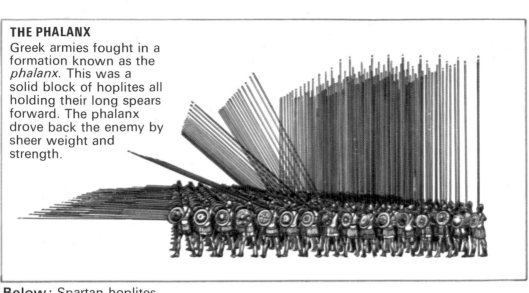

Below: Spartan hoplites being trained for battle, well protected by armour, helmets and shields. They are learning to hold formation in the phalanx and to skirmish.

The Roman world

Rome, beginning as a small town on the banks of the River Tiber, grew to rule one of the mightiest empires the world has ever seen. According to legend Rome was started in 753 BC by Romulus and Remus. In the 3rd century BC Rome conquered its main rival, Carthage.

Under great commanders such as Julius Caesar (102–44 BC) much of Europe was conquered. At the height of its power the Roman Empire stretched from Spain to the Caspian Sea, from Egypt to the North of England.

The army

Every man was obliged to serve in the army, which was made up of *legions*. Each legion had about 5,000 men, made up of groups of 100 commanded by *centurions*. At first only Roman citizens served in the legions, but later non-Romans were allowed into their ranks.

The legionary

The early legionary wore a coat of mail and a bronze helmet rather like a peaked cap worn back to front, which had two large cheek pieces to protect the face. He carried a large, almost oval-shaped shield.

Later his equipment was improved and the legionary in the 1st century AD had a helmet of iron with a front peak and a wide spreading neck guard. Two wide cheek pieces were tied under the chin. On top of the helmet he

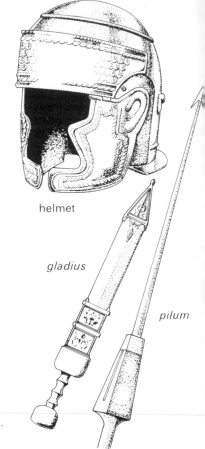

helmet

gladius

pilum

Above: equipment of the Roman soldier.
Below: a fight to the death between gladiators.

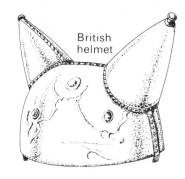

British helmet

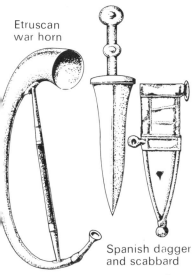

Etruscan war horn

Spanish dagger and scabbard

Above: equipment of some of Rome's enemies.
Below: Roman troops attack the city walls.

could fix a small crest of feathers or horsehair.

His body was protected by a very clever arrangement of metal plates fitted to leather straps. His large shield, or *scutum*, was rectangular and slightly curved.

Roman weapons

The training of a legionary was hard and he had to learn the use of many weapons. His sword (*gladius*) had a wide blade but was quite short with a sharp point.

His other weapon was the *pilum*, which was a long spear with a wooden shaft. The point was at the end of a long metal arm of fairly soft iron.

Battle tactics

In battle the legion usually formed itself into three long lines of troops and advanced towards the enemy. On command they stopped and all threw their spears at the same moment. If the spear missed and stuck in the ground or a shield, the soft iron neck bent, so making it difficult to pull out or to throw back at the Romans. After throwing the *pilum* the Romans drew their swords and moved forward, protected by their shields.

The Roman legion sometimes used a special shield arrangement known as 'the tortoise' or *testudo*. Men in the front ranks held their shields before them; those at the sides guarded the flanks whilst others held their shields above their heads. In this way the whole group was covered by a wall of shields and could advance right up to a wall or gate with little risk.

The Dark Ages

For hundreds of years the Roman army kept the frontiers of the empire safe from invaders. However, the Roman empire began to break up and during the 4th and 5th centuries fierce tribes swept into Western Europe from the east in search of land and plunder.

Barbarian invasions and new kingdoms

The Huns were ferocious nomads from central Asia. Hordes of their warriors swept on horseback through Russia and Europe, and in turn pushed other tribes such as the Visigoths and Ostrogoths before them.

A group of tribes known as Franks conquered much of West and Central Europe giving their name to modern France. When the Romans left Britain, Angles and Saxons invaded and settled there, forming a number of kingdoms.

The Vikings

In the 8th century a new series of raids began and these were the work of the Vikings. These brave, fearless seamen came from Scandinavia—Norway, Sweden and Denmark. They believed that if they died heroically they would go to *Valhalla*, the warrior's heaven.

Their *longships* with square, striped sails and rows of oars, took them along the coasts of Europe and along rivers to London, Paris and right to the heart of Russia.

Viking weapons

Their circular shields were made of wood with a small central metal dome to protect the hand which held on to a bar at the back.

One of the Vikings' favourite weapons was the long handled axe. The head had a broad edge and the handle was up to two metres long and held with two hands.

Viking swords had long, straight blades with only a small point and were used to slash rather than stab. At the top of the blade and base of the grip was a metal bar which protected the hand holding the sword.

Viking armour

Some, but not all, Vikings owned a coat of mail. Their helmets were often very simple, just covering the top of the head, but others had face guards.

This fearsome helmet dates from the 9th century. It was found in a Saxon burial ship at Sutton Hoo, England.

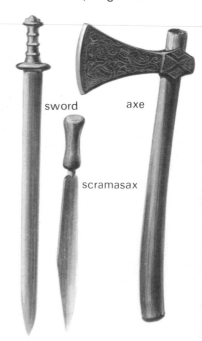

sword   axe

scramasax

Weapons of the Vikings. Knives and swords were used for slashing rather than stabbing.

Viking raiders soon discovered that churches and monasteries held rich treasures and often raided them. The sight of their longships filled coastal and river settlements with dread.

The Normans

Some Vikings (or 'Northmen') settled in the north of France, which became known as Normandy. In 1066 under their leader, Duke William, the Normans carried out the great invasion of England which started with the Battle of Hastings.

William claimed that the English throne was really his and that Harold, the king, had no right to it. William gathered together an army of knights and their followers and in October 1066 set sail to land near Hastings in Southern England.

Norman knights

Most of William's soldiers were horsemen. They carried a long, kite-shaped shield of wood and leather with straps to hold it on the arm or hang around the neck. They wore long mail shirts reaching to the knees and split back and front so that they could ride comfortably.

On their heads were conical helmets with a broad bar,

The Normans soon controlled Britain. Most Norman warriors were horsemen and wore mail tunics and helmets.

Each link of mail was joined with four others and rivetted together.

Norman helmets were conical, with a bar to protect the nose and face.

known as the *nasal*, covering the nose. They fought with sword or lance which they held either tucked under the arm, or in the hand, to stab with.

The Battle of Hastings

Harold's men, tired after a previous battle at York and a long march south, took up position on top of a small hill. They fought with swords and long-handled axes and held their round, wooden shields in front of them to make a wooden wall. Few had any armour.

The Normans attacked but were at a disadvantage since they had to charge uphill. The English held their positions and resisted several attacks until they broke their lines and ran down the hill. The Norman horsemen then turned on them and caused many casualties.

The defeat of Harold

The English reformed their battered lines but the Norman archers rained arrows on them. In one charge Harold was struck down and the battle was lost. William, Duke of Normandy, was now William the Conqueror, King of England.

The Crusades

In medieval times the Islamic civilization of the Arabs and Turks covered most of the Middle East, North Africa and much of Spain. Jerusalem, a holy city for Moslems, Christians and Jews, was held by Turks.

At that time it was the custom for the Christians of Europe to go on a pilgrimage to the Holy Land. They were sometimes mistreated by the Turks, who were known to them as Saracens.

Holy wars

In 1095 Pope Urban preached that it was wrong for the Holy Land to be ruled by people who were not Christians. He called upon everybody to join together in a holy 'war of the cross' or *crusade*.

This was the beginning of the First Crusade. Between the 11th and 14th centuries there were many other Crusades.

The fight for Jerusalem

The First Crusade was probably the most successful for the Crusaders, who drove out the Turks from most of the Holy Land. A Christian Kingdom was set up there and the Crusaders built great castles to protect their new lands.

Soon they began quarrelling among themselves and despite a Second Crusade, in 1147, before long the Moslems

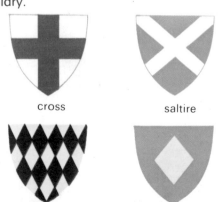

Above: Saracens wore little armour and had round shields. They were expert archers and horsemen.

Below: knights began to use simple badges like these so that they could be recognized in battle. This was the start of heraldry.

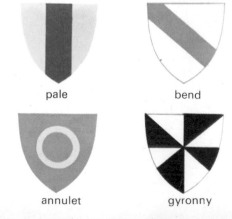

cross

saltire

pale

bend

fusilly

lozenge

annulet

gyronny

were again in control.

In 1187 the great Saracen warrior Saladin re-captured Jerusalem. Two years later a Third Crusade set out with three kings to lead it: Frederick Barbarossa from Germany, Philip of France and Richard the Lion Heart of England. Frederick was drowned on the way; Philip and Richard carried on but failed to take Jerusalem.

Armour

The Turks wore little armour but relied on small, fast horses to make quick raids before the Crusaders on their heavy horses were able to take action.

The Crusaders wore thick, padded coats under mail shirts, and mail leggings. Some had metal plates fitted at their knees. Over their mail many wore a white tunic with a red cross as a badge. Helmets now covered the head complately and in order to recognize people crests and badges (*heraldic devices*) were worn.

Orders of knights

Some groups of Christian knights were rather like fighting monks, such as the Order of the Knights of St. John, or the Knights Templar, who guarded the pilgrims on their journey. These knights made promises to live Christian lives. Later they became powerful and greedy, and forgot their promises.

Above: a Knight Hospitaller, one of the special orders of Christian knights in the Holy Land.

Below: heraldry became more complicated. These are the coats of arms (or family badges) of famous Crusaders. Heraldry is still in use today.

Frederick
Barbarossa

Richard
the Lion Heart

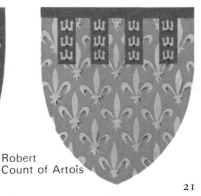

Robert
Count of Artois

Knights in armour

An army of the late 15th century retreats from the battlefield. The knights wear armour in the Gothic style. The footsoldier (right) wears the popular kettle hat.

In late medieval times the son of a nobleman would have to serve as a *page* and then as a *squire* before he could be knighted. He would then promise to behave honourably as a knight and receive the *accolade* which made him a knight—a tap on the shoulder with the flat of a sword.

Plate armour

Towards the end of the 12th century small metal plates were being attached to the knight's mail shirts and leggings at the points of greatest danger. More and more plates were used: by about 1400 the knight was compately covered by plate armour.

The plates were carefully shaped and placed so as to stop and turn away the cut or thrust of a blade. They were fastened to leather straps and arranged to allow easy movement.

Wearing armour

The knight first put on a padded garment with patches of mail sewn at the armpits and elbows. Over this *arming doublet* he might have a coat of mail, and over that his plate armour—leg pieces, cuirass, arm pieces, helmet and gauntlets, all held on by straps or laces.

Armour was not very heavy although it was hot and stuffy to wear. A knight could ride, fight and run quite easily on the battlefield.

Knights in England and France would send to towns such as Nuremberg, Augsburg or Solingen in Germany, Milan in Italy, or Innsbruck in Austria, to buy the best quality armour.

Foot soldiers and archers

The ordinary foot soldier was not so well equipped. The armour he wore was probably what he could capture in battle. Often his only protection was a padded coat, and his only weapon a farm tool on a pole.

By the late thirteenth century the English were using large numbers of archers. The Battles of Crécy (1346), Poitiers (1356) and Agincourt (1415) were won by the longbow. The crossbow was stronger and its bolts could penetrate plate armour, but it was very slow to reload. Firearms (*see p. 25*) began to be of great importance.

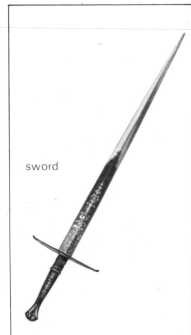

sword

A 15th century knight's long sword of war with its scabbard. Note the long *quillons* (cross guard).

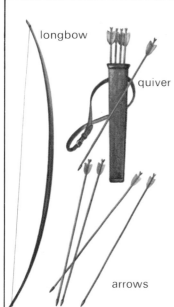

longbow

quiver

arrows

The metre-long arrow from a longbow could easily pierce mail or armour.

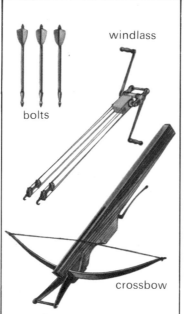

windlass

bolts

crossbow

Some crossbows were so strong that a windlass was used to pull back the cord.

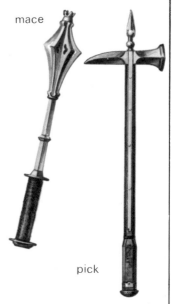

mace

pick

In hand to hand combat knights often used an axe, a mace or a pick to deal a blow.

From armour to guns

In the 16th century the armourer's skill reached its height. But in the great wars of the time armour proved less and less defence against firearms.

Styles of armour

One style of armour popular until about 1530 is known as *Maximilian armour*, after the Emperor of Austria. Pieces of this armour had ridges to give strength as well as to turn away the point of a weapon. The helmet completely covered the head, and was known as a *close helm*.

Greenwich armour was produced at the armoury of Henry VIII of England, set up in 1515.

Tournaments and parades

For centuries knights enjoyed practising their skills with weapons. Mock fights between groups of knights were called *tournaments*. When two knights fought each other this was known as the *joust* or *tilt*. Specially strong armour was worn for the tilt.

Some suits of armour were made to be worn only for ceremonies and parades. They were fine examples of craftsmanship, but would have been little use in battle as their finely decorated surfaces would have caught and held a sword or axe blade instead of turning it away.

Swords

As armour was now very strong and well designed, ordinary swords could not pierce it. Swords were made with a hilt big enough to be held in two hands, so that a really powerful blow could be struck. Other swords had long, thin, strong blades, which could stab at any places not covered by armour.

Some armour, like this made in Augsburg, in 1520, was only worn for parades. Its style imitates civilian fashion, and would be of little use on the battlefield.

This beautifully decorated matchlock rifle was made in Germany in 1598. As guns became more common, the use of armour grew less.

Early firearms

Gunpowder, an explosive mixture of charcoal, sulphur and saltpetre, was used by the Chinese over nine centuries ago, but it did not reach Europe until the Middle Ages. The first guns we know of, in the early 14th century, were simple cannons, used to break down fortifications. Soon small handguns were being made, crude barrels fastened to a wooden *stock*. They were very inaccurate.

Matchlock muskets

Gradually handguns improved. By the late 16th century many soldiers had *matchlock* muskets. These had long barrels and were loaded by pouring gunpowder, followed by a lead ball, down the barrel of the musket.

To fire the gun, a glowing piece of cord, the *match*, attached to a moving arm called a *serpentine*, was touched into some powder placed in a small pan at the side of the barrel near the close end, the gun's *breech*.

This pan was next to the *touch hole*, which was drilled through the side of the barrel. When the match touched the powder in the pan, it flared up and the flame passed through the touch hole to set off the main charge of powder and so blow out the bullet.

The decline of armour

Armour which was strong enough to stop a bullet was thick and heavy. Soldiers felt it was better to risk a wound than to wear heavy armour in battle. At first they began to leave off the leg plates and wore long, leather boots instead. Later the arm defences were left off, but most troops kept their helmets and breast and back plates and so remained fairly well protected whilst being freer to move.

Sometimes knights took part in foot combat using the poleaxe.

A small Spanish army with firearms easily defeated the poorly armed Incas.

The new armies

In the seventeenth century Europe was torn apart by long and bitter wars. The Thirty Years War (1618-1648) was a struggle between Catholic and Protestant forces that spread over most of the continent. At the end of it Germany was in ruins, and many people were left homeless and starving. In Britain there was civil war between Parliament and King Charles I lasting from 1642-49.

Organized armies

During this century armies were better organized and trained. In Sweden Gustavus Adolphus was training his armies to fight in units all dressed in the same uniform.

The army of the French King Louis XIV was organized into permanent regiments in this century. In Britain, Oliver Cromwell re-organized his Parliamentarian (or 'Roundhead') army on similar lines. The men were well trained, drilled, and disciplined.

Cromwellian arms and armour

The cavalrymen of Cromwell's 'New Model Army', as it was known, were fitted with a helmet which had a wide neck guard, cheek pieces and a peak with a nasal bar that protected nose and face.

Troopers wore breast and back plates and a gauntlet which reached to the elbow. They were armed with a sword and a pair of pistols. The infantry carried a long matchlock musket, whilst other units were armed with long pikes. Pikemen protected the musketeers while they re-loaded.

The big problem with matchlock muskets was that they were easily put out of action by bad weather, for the wind could blow away the powder in the pan or rain could put out the match or damp the powder.

The wheellock

Early in the 16th century a new system of firing guns had been invented—the *wheellock*. Sparks made by a metal wheel rubbing against a piece of mineral called pyrites fired the powder in the pan. The wheellock worked very well but it was expensive to make and a little complicated. If it jammed or broke it was often difficult to repair.

Above: a trooper of Cromwell's New Model Army wears a helmet with a faceguard.

Below: a musketeer loads his matchlock and pushes down a bullet with his ramrod.

Pistols

The wheellock could be made to any size so that it was possible to fit it to small firearms and so the first pistols were made. Cavalrymen of the seventeenth century usually carried a pair of pistols in holsters at the front of the saddle.

Fencing

Late in the 15th century a new type of sword, the *rapier*, had been developed. It had a long, narrow blade and the hilt had metal bars to protect the hand. The rapier was a weapon designed to stab rather than cut and a new style of fighting, using this sword, was developed in the 16th and 17th centuries. This was called *fencing*.

Rapiers and daggers

Sometimes the fencer used two rapiers, one in each hand, or a sword in one and a dagger in the other. The dagger was held in the left hand and was used to catch or parry an opponent's blade. Instead of bars some rapiers had metal dishes or cups to protect the hand. These were especially popular in Spain.

Smallswords

In the late seventeenth century the rapier was made smaller and became more a town or dress sword. These *smallswords* were often very pretty with decorated hilts, sometimes of precious metals. Smallswords were worn by most gentlemen in Britain until about the 1780's.

Below: two Spanish gentlemen fight a duel with left-handed daggers and cup-hilted rapiers. The dagger was used to catch or parry the blade of an opponent's sword. Duels were fought over matters of honour, often to the death.

With the rapier, swordplay became a fine art. Fencing was often taught in special schools, and to become a good swordsman required great skill.

Redcoats and rebels

By the eighteenth century France and Great Britain had become very powerful. Both were building empires and fought each other in India and North America.

It was also an age of rebellion and revolution. Scottish supporters of the Stuart royal family ('Jacobites') rebelled against England in 1715 and 1745. From 1775–83 American colonists fought Britain for their independence. The French Revolution took place in 1789.

Armies

The armies of 18th century Europe were made up of professional, uniformed soldiers. Discipline was very harsh, especially in the army of Prussia. Many men were forced to become soldiers against their will.

Bayonets

Infantry officers and cavalry still used swords, but by the middle of the century most troops had given them up, and relied on the long knife called the *bayonet*.

The hilt of the bayonet was pushed into the muzzle of the musket so that it could be used like a spear. Later a socket was developed so that the musket could be fired even if the bayonet was in place.

The flintlock

Most soldiers carried some kind of firearm. Infantry continued to use the long-barrelled musket and the cavalry

Jacobite (1745)

French revolutionary (1790)

American revolutionary (1777)

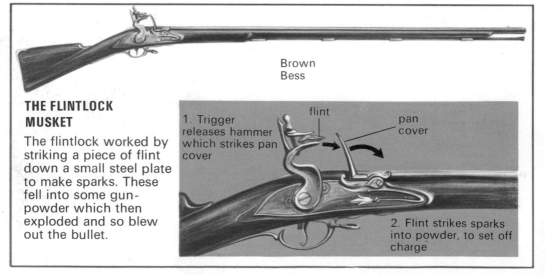

Brown Bess

THE FLINTLOCK MUSKET

The flintlock worked by striking a piece of flint down a small steel plate to make sparks. These fell into some gunpowder which then exploded and so blew out the bullet.

1. Trigger releases hammer which strikes pan cover

flint

pan cover

2. Flint strikes sparks into powder, to set off charge

sometimes carried a short gun called a *carbine* in addition to their pistols. These were fired by means of a *flintlock*, which had been invented early in the 17th century.

To load a flintlock either a paper cartridge or a powder horn could be used. A pinch of powder was put into the pan and the cover closed. The rest of the powder was poured down the barrel and a lead ball and wad were then pushed down with a long thin *ramrod*.

Muskets and rifles

The British infantry were armed with a flintlock musket known as the 'Brown Bess'. It was a fine weapon, but it did not shoot very straight.

When the British 'Redcoats' were at war with the American colonists, they were amazed at the accuracy and range of the Pennsylvanian Long Rifle. In a *rifled* barrel, spiral grooves make the bullet spin and this keeps it on course, and so it is much more accurate.

Bullets were made by melting lead and pouring it into a specially shaped metal mould. When the lead cooled and set hard, the mould was opened and the balls of lead removed.

Blunderbusses and pistols

A popular weapon of this century was the blunderbuss. Its wide muzzle could fire up to twenty bullets at once.

Duels, once fought with swords, were now fought with pistols. Specially made pairs of pistols, together with all the tools, were sold in cases.

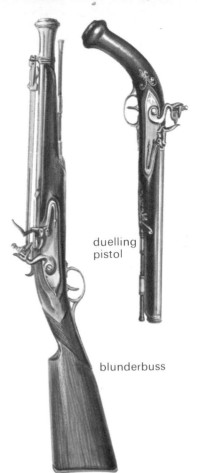

duelling pistol

blunderbuss

Below: in 1759 British troops captured Quebec in Canada from the French.

The age of empires

At the beginning of the nineteenth century France, under Napoleon, was still at war with Great Britain. At the Battle of Waterloo in 1815 France was beaten, and Britain went on to build its empire, fighting in several continents.

France and Britain were allies in the Crimean War against Russia (1854–56). In North America the Civil War broke out in 1861 between northern and southern states. The century ended with bitter fighting in South Africa, as Britain fought the Dutch settlers, or Boers.

Percussion firing

This was an age of great scientific and technical advances. New machinery meant that the making of weapons was no longer the job of one craftsman.

New inventions enabled factories to produce weapons in great numbers and there were many new features in firearm design. Early in the century the percussion system of firing was introduced.

Another new idea was the use of metal cartridges which were loaded in at the breech end. The *cartridge*, a case containing a charge of powder and a bullet, had previously been made of paper or cloth, and had been loaded in from the muzzle.

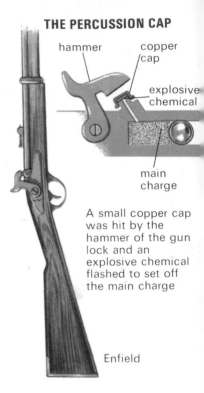

THE PERCUSSION CAP

hammer

copper cap

explosive chemical

main charge

A small copper cap was hit by the hammer of the gun lock and an explosive chemical flashed to set off the main charge

Enfield

Above: the percussion cap was much simpler than the flintlock.

Below: the Royal Small Arms Factory, Enfield, during the Boer War.

Colt revolvers

In 1836 an American, Samuel Colt, had designed a simple, but very good, percussion *revolver*. The revolver was a pistol with a cylinder which revolved, so that one could fire several shots without reloading. He improved the design and set up a factory to make the revolver. Colt revolvers became very popular and several kinds were made. The firm is still making firearms today, including one first introduced in 1873.

Automatic pistols

By the end of this century firearm designers had invented several self-loading pistols. A container or *magazine* holding a number of cartridges was loaded into the pistol and each time the trigger was pressed a shot was fired.

At the same time the empty case was thrown out and a fresh cartridge was loaded into the breech ready for the next shot. This action could be repeated until all the cartridges in the magazine had been used up.

Machine guns

There had been several guns which would fire for as long as ammunition was fed in but they had all been worked by hand. In 1883 Sir Hiram Maxim invented a gun which was fully automatic.

When the trigger was pressed the gun started to fire and went on firing until the trigger was released, the ammunition ran out, or the gun jammed.

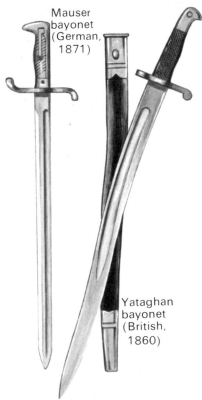

Mauser bayonet (German, 1871)

Yataghan bayonet (British, 1860)

Above: most troops carried some kind of bayonet.
Below: soldiers' uniforms of the 19th century.

Russian infantry (1854)

US (Union) cavalry (1861)

British infantry (1880)

The Wild West

When the colonists began to move across North America they came into conflict with the American Indians who lived there. There were many battles between the Indians and the soldiers and settlers who invaded their land.

The Indians were excellent horsemen and were brilliant at making sudden raids. They used bows and flint-headed arrows, lances, clubs and a kind of axe called a *tomahawk*. They soon began to buy, steal or capture firearms.

Many famous guns such as the Colt revolver and the Winchester lever-action repeating rifle were in use during this period. Many men also carried a fighting knife, known as the *Bowie knife*.

Colt single action
army revolver (1873)

Winchester
repeating
rifle (1873)

Warriors of the world

We have seen how some weapons were often discovered in one part of the world long before they were used in another.

South America

When the Spanish first landed in Central and Southern America the natives had never seen firearms, armour or horses. Their weapons were generally much simpler. A popular one was a *maquahuilt* which was a flat, wooden club with pieces of sharp stone fitted along the edge.

Bows and arrows were used and in the jungle the natives used blow-pipes and poisoned darts. Clubs and shields of animal skin and wood were often decorated with feathers and painted.

Another weapon used to capture animals was the *bolas*, which consisted of three weighted balls fitted at the end of three leather thongs or ropes tied together at the centre. These were whirled round the head and then released.

India

An Indian warrior usually wore a simple round helmet fitted with a mail curtain to protect the neck and back of the head. He also wore a coat of mail or covered his body with plates of armour.

His weapons were usually some kind of sword, often with a curved blade, a dagger and perhaps a short lance. Many warriors used bows and arrows and maces with spiked heads were quite common. Shields of animal hide or metal were usually round and decorated.

When the knowledge of gunpowder reached India the weapon makers produced many matchlock and flintlock muskets but very few pistols.

Above: Aztec warriors carried round shields and were armed with stone edged wooden clubs.
Below: elephants were used by Indian armies as a kind of tank to carry warriors into battle.

Japan

From Japan came some of the finest swords ever made anywhere in the world. The blades were brightly polished, slightly curved and had a cutting edge that was so sharp that it could cut through metal.

The warrior who carried the sword was known as a Samurai and he wore armour which was very different from that of Europe. It was made up of tiny pieces of metal covered with black lacquer—a kind of paint—and then laced together with brightly coloured silk braid into larger pieces. These pieces were then tied to the body.

The helmet was often fitted with tall, exciting crests.

Japanese bows were very long, over two metres, and were held, not at the middle, but about one third of the way up. Their arrows were long and were fitted with many different points.

Above: this Japanese Samurai armour is made of small plates laced together. The helmet includes a fierce face mask.

Below: this painting of a Zulu chief was made over a century ago. He owns a shield, short spears and a knobkerry.

Africa

In the north of Africa the Arabs used muskets and flintlock pistols as well as swords. In central and southern Africa the spear and the dagger were more common. In the Sudan shields were usually round and made of rhinoceros or hippopotamus hide, and the sword was sometimes carried in a sheath made from the skin of a crocodile.

One of the bravest warriors of nineteenth century Africa was the Zulu. He carried a large shield made of cowhide and used a short spear called an *assegai*, which he could throw or use for stabbing. His other weapon was the *knobkerry*, which was a short club with a round knob at the end. When the Zulus fought they were formed into regiments (*impis*).

Curious weapons

There have been many strange weapons; some were designed to do two jobs. There were many swords with pistols fitted to the hilts and there was even a breast-plate fitted with some pistols.

Other pistols were so small that they could be held inside the fist with the barrel sticking out between the fingers. Some weapons were disguised, such as purses with pistols fitted inside them or a Japanese fan which concealed a pistol.

Some weapons were of unusual design, like the quoit used by the Sikhs of India.

This was a flat metal ring with a sharpened edge. When sent spinning through the air, it could give a very nasty wound to the enemy.

Some weapons were designed to scare the enemy as much as injure them. The fearful sound made by the Japanese whistling arrows must have made the enemy want to run away as much as the actual arrows.

Often weapons are purely ornamental, and are meant to impress rather than injure. For example modern military officers still wear finely decorated swords on ceremonial occasions, although the sword is no longer used in modern warfare.

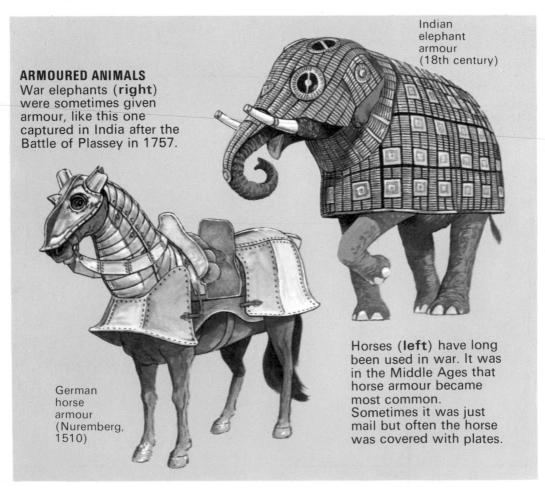

Indian elephant armour (18th century)

ARMOURED ANIMALS
War elephants (**right**) were sometimes given armour, like this one captured in India after the Battle of Plassey in 1757.

German horse armour (Nuremberg, 1510)

Horses (**left**) have long been used in war. It was in the Middle Ages that horse armour became most common. Sometimes it was just mail but often the horse was covered with plates.

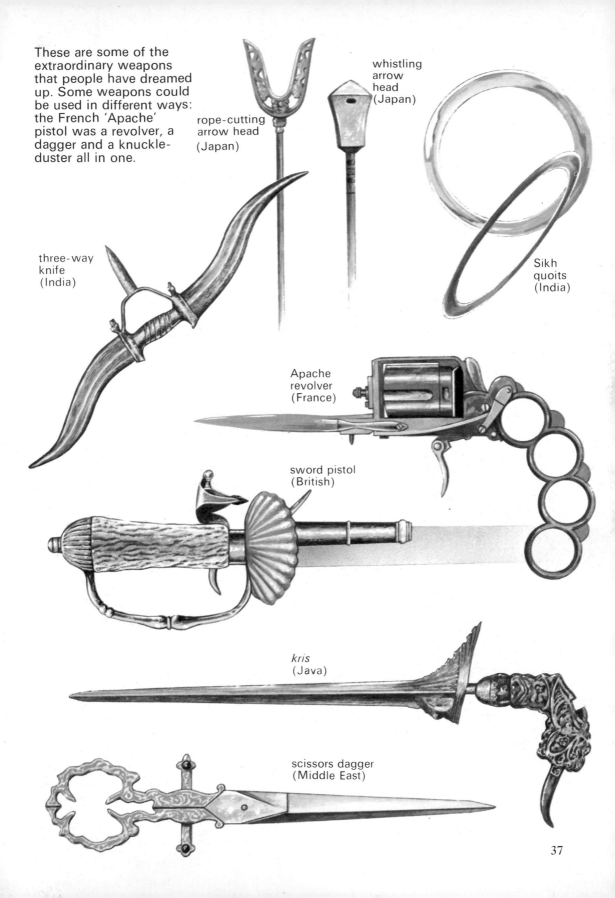

These are some of the extraordinary weapons that people have dreamed up. Some weapons could be used in different ways: the French 'Apache' pistol was a revolver, a dagger and a knuckle-duster all in one.

rope-cutting arrow head (Japan)

whistling arrow head (Japan)

three-way knife (India)

Sikh quoits (India)

Apache revolver (France)

sword pistol (British)

kris (Java)

scissors dagger (Middle East)

World War One

At the beginning of this century Britain, France, Germany and Russia were the most powerful countries in the world. Each of the great powers had made agreements with other countries that should any trouble break out, then they would help each other.

The outbreak of war

In June 1914 the Austrian archduke and his wife were killed by a gunman. Austria blamed a small country called Serbia. They called for Russian help, and soon the whole of Europe was embroiled in one of the most terrible wars ever known.

On one side were Great Britain, France, the troops of their empires, Russia, Japan, and eventually the United States. On the other side were Germany, Italy, Austria and Turkey. Soon over twenty countries were at war.

The extent of the war

Great battles were fought in France, Belgium, Russia, Italy, Africa and Turkey. Millions of men were killed and wounded. For the first time civilians were called up to join the army in large numbers. Women worked as nurses and made ammunition in factories.

At sea there were very few big battles but submarines sank many ships. In the air, for the first time aeroplanes and airships were used to bomb targets as well as to photograph enemy positions.

Germany surrenders

The war lasted for more than four years, causing tremendous damage and misery. Germany and her allies were finally forced to surrender and the war ended on November 11th 1918.

British troops with steel helmets and rifles leave their trench.

German snipers: their spiked helmets were later replaced by steel ones.

Trench warfare

Much of the fighting during the war was in France, with both armies in deep trenches which zigzagged across the countryside. These trenches were protected in front by great lines of barbed wire and the ground between the front line trenches was called 'No-man's-land'.

In wet weather the ground became a sea of mud so deep in places that men and animals were drowned in it.

Steel helmets

Because the troops spent so much time in the trenches they often received head injuries. Heavy artillery would pound the trenches, pouring shells into the enemy positions. First the French and then the British and Germans designed steel helmets to wear in the trenches and these saved many lives.

Weapons

The troops, who lived in terrible discomfort in the trenches, were armed with repeating rifles, bayonets and their officers carried revolvers or automatic pistols.

One of the most important weapons of the war was the machine gun which all armies now had. New weapons which it was hoped would be able to break through the lines of trenches were introduced.

Poison gas

Poison gas was first introduced by the Germans in 1916 and troops then had to be fitted with special masks so that they could breath safely. Even so, many troops were horribly injured by breathing in gas.

Tanks

The British introduced the tank, which was a vehicle covered with armour and fitted with special caterpillar tracks so that it could cross even the roughest ground with ease.

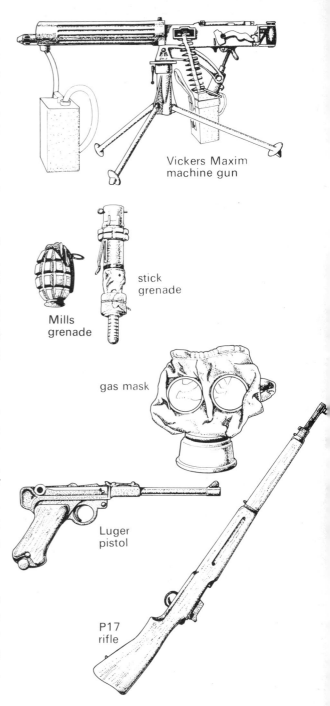

Vickers Maxim machine gun

stick grenade

Mills grenade

gas mask

Luger pistol

P17 rifle

Weapons of World War One: in this war there were many repeating weapons like the Vickers machine gun and the German Luger pistol. Small bombs (grenades) were used a great deal, as was poison gas.

60-mm
bazooka
(US)

76-mm
mortar
(British)

Special weapons like the
bazooka and mortar could
knock out tanks.

World War Two

When peace came in 1918 it did not last. A new leader, Adolf Hitler, seized power in Germany. Germany invaded other countries including Austria and Czechoslovakia. In August 1939, she attacked Poland, and France and Britain declared war on Germany. The Second World War had started. It lasted until 1945 and many countries took part, including the USSR, the USA, Italy and Japan.

Weapons of the war

One of the most important weapons of the war was the tank and the Germans were experts in its use. There were different types of tank including some very fast, light ones as well as very heavy, thickly armoured ones.

Special anti-tank guns were designed to knock them out. Aircraft played a very big part in all the battles, being used to bomb troops, factories, bridges and cities. Special, fast, high flying planes photographed enemy positions and small heavily armoured fighters tried to stop the bombers as well as attacking enemy ground forces and transport.

Infantrymen carried light machine guns as well as rifles and such weapons as mortars which could throw a small bomb quite a distance.

Radar, rockets and bombs

One very important new invention was called *Radar*. It used radio waves to find targets and could locate them over 300 kilometres away. Other new weapons such as long distance rockets and flying bombs were also used. Bombs reduced the cities of Europe to rubble, and every citizen of the countries at war now found themselves in the front line.

The atomic bomb

Britain and America had succeded in making the most powerful weapon ever, the atomic bomb, and in 1945 used it twice on Japan. Hundreds of thousands were killed and many died a slow death from the dreadful sickness caused by radiation. Warfare was no longer a matter of fighting between small groups of soldiers. Nobody was safe from attack, no matter where they were.

On D-Day, 6 June 1944, British, American and other allied troops landed on the Normandy coast.

The modern world

Since the end of World War Two in 1945, new technology and scientific inventions have been used to make weapons even more powerful. The USA, fighting in Vietnam in the 1960's and early 1970's developed new and deadly weapons, as did many other countries.

Firearms

In place of the older, heavy, ten-shot rifle most troops now carry a light, self-loading rifle or sub-machine gun. It is made of plastic, aluminium or steel and has a magazine which holds thirty or more rounds.

Cartridges are smaller, but some are so powerful that they can drive a bullet right through the engine of a car or thick steel plate.

Sights

In the past, darkness gave soldiers the chance to move secretly but this is no longer the case. Light intensifiers and infra-red sights can show up a man or vehicle even in total darkness.

A special lamp which gives a light beam called a *laser* can be fitted to weapons. The firer sees a red dot and, when this is on the target, presses the trigger and cannot miss. These lasers can also be used to aim bombs and rockets. Weapons are in use that until now were only dreamed of in science fiction stories.

helmet
visor
flak jacket
truncheon
plastic shield

Above: for riot control, today's soldier again uses shield and armour.
Below: S. Vietnamese troops launch an attack from a US helicopter.

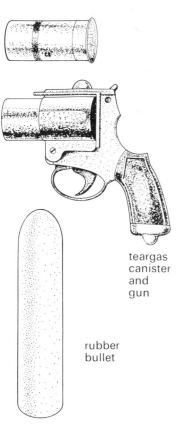

teargas
canister
and
gun

rubber
bullet

Above: tear gas and rubber bullets are used to disperse crowds.

Below: a soldier takes aim with a light-intensifying sight.

Modern armour

Tanks are still very important and new materials have been used to make armour which is stronger but lighter than the older forms. The shape has been improved so that the tank is low on the ground and is therefore a much harder target to hit.

Special kinds of anti-tank ammunition have been developed to increase the chances of knocking out tanks. Some shells have special heads that will penetrate the thickest armour.

Rockets and missiles

Many countries now possess the atom and hydrogen bombs as well as chemical and germ warfare devices. In germ warfare, dangerous germs would be released amongst the enemy to infect them. Some of this could be sent against an enemy by means of guided missiles and rockets with a range of several thousand kilometres.

Satellites far above the earth can be used to steer these missiles as well as keeping watch on an enemy's movements. Special killer satellites and lasers are being developed which will knock out an enemy's satellites.

The future

Modern weapons are now so powerful that if they were used the world could be so seriously damaged that men would be unable to survive. From the simple weapons of wood and stone have developed frightening weapons of total destruction.

Books to read

Arms and Armour, Wilkinson; A & C Black 1963
The Roman Army, Connolly; Macdonald Educational 1975
The Greek Armies, Connolly; Macdonald Educational 1977
Hannibal and the Enemies of Rome, Connolly; Macdonald Educational 1978
Knights and the Crusades, Gibson; Macdonald Educational 1975
World War One, Hoare; Macdonald Educational 1973
World War Two, Unstead; Macdonald Educational 1973
Let's look at Arms and Armour, Wilkinson; Muller 1968
Medieval Warfare, Hindley; Wayland 1971

Things to do

Model making is fun: there are many very good plastic kits of soldiers of different ages. There are also several figures which can be dressed in many different uniforms. You can also buy sets of small figures to make up complete armies.
Collecting is another possibility: many stamps feature pictures of soldiers and sailors. Other stamps have battle scenes.

You might like to look around for some military buttons and cap badges which are still quite cheap. There are some shops which sell military surplus uniforms and you could perhaps get some uniform parts.
Often the Services put on shows at local fairs: look out for these. There are some clubs and societies which put on mock battles and tournaments. There are also wargame clubs and these have battles with model soldiers. There may be one near you.

Places to go

These museums have some arms and armour on show:
Aberdeen
Aberdeen University Anthropological Museum
Birmingham
City Museum and Art Gallery
Bolton
Museum and Art Gallery
Bristol
City Museum
Cambridge
Fitzwilliam Museum
Chester
Grosvenor Museum
King Charles' Tower
Colchester
Colchester and Essex Museum
Dundee
Art Galleries
Broughty Castle Museum

Edinburgh
Royal Scottish Museum
National Museum of Antiquities of Scotland
Glasgow
Art Gallery and Museum
Old Glasgow Museum
Guernsey
Castle Cornet
Leeds
Abbey House Museum
Leicester
The Magazine
Lewes
Anne of Cleves House
Liverpool
City Museum
London
Artillery Museum
British Museum
Hampton Court Palace
Imperial War Museum
London Museum
National Maritime Museum
Tower of London
Victoria and Albert Museum
Wallace Collection
Maidstone
Museum and Art Gallery
Manchester
City Art Gallery
Newcastle-upon-Tyne
John G. Joicey Museum
The Keep Museum
Laing Art Gallery and Museum
Museum of Antiquities
Norwich
Castle Museum
Strangers Hall
Oxford
Pitt Rivers Museum
York
Castle Museum